AN UNLIKELY ASTRONAUT

BY ASTRONAUT SUSAN KILRAIN

WITH FRANCIS FRENCH

ILLUSTRATED BY BECKY HARDY

Growing Up with Brothers

Susan grew up in Georgia in the 1960s with three boisterous brothers. They made fun of Susan's ears that stuck out far from her head. "Fly, Dumbo, fly!" the boys yelled as she stood on top of the family car. Tears rolled down Susan's cheeks as her brothers teased her. They didn't know that she dreamed of soaring high in the sky. Yet it seemed unlikely that Susan would ever fly.

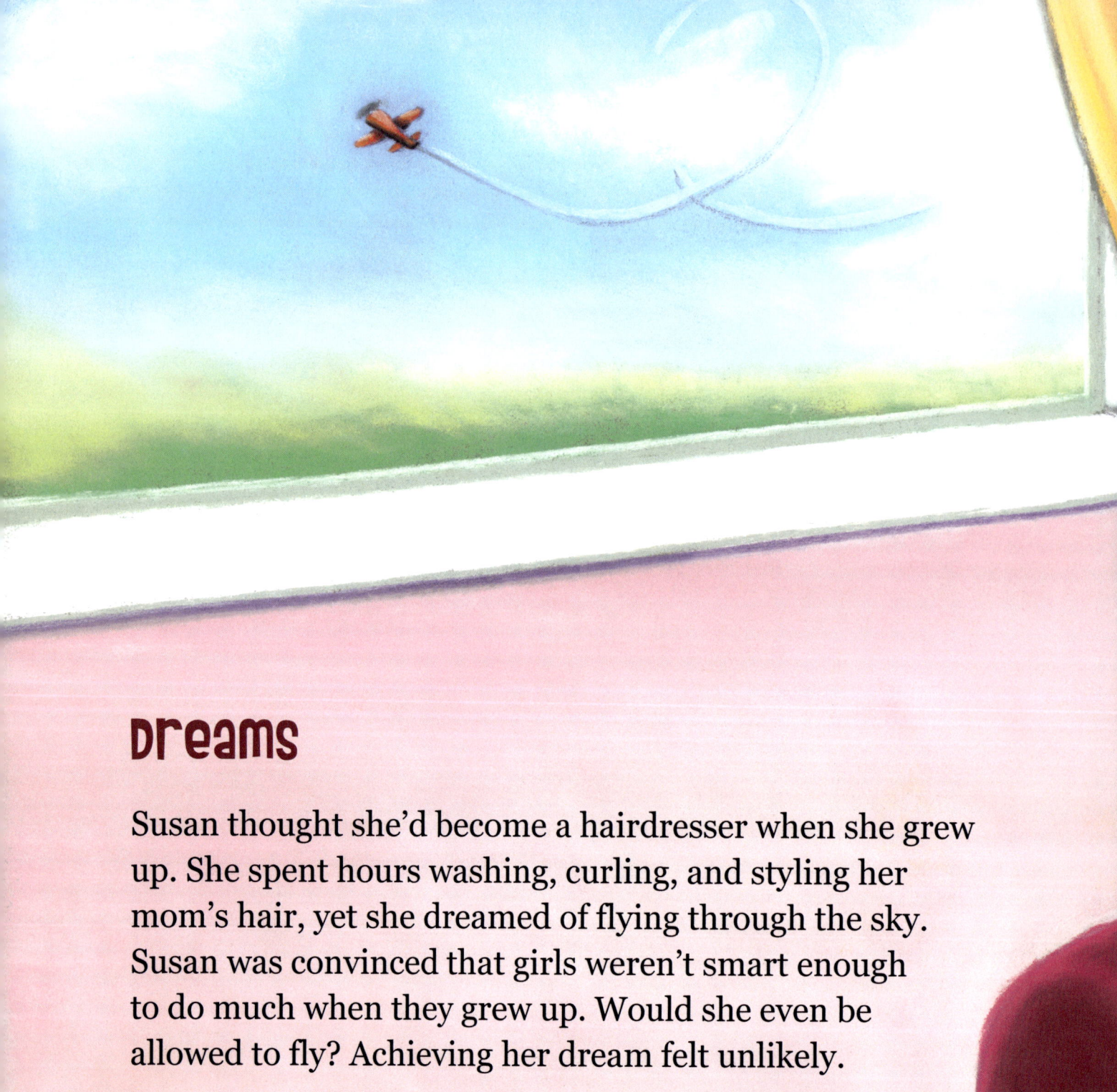

Dreams

Susan thought she'd become a hairdresser when she grew up. She spent hours washing, curling, and styling her mom's hair, yet she dreamed of flying through the sky. Susan was convinced that girls weren't smart enough to do much when they grew up. Would she even be allowed to fly? Achieving her dream felt unlikely.

Watching the Airplanes

Susan's family didn't have much money, so they didn't take vacations or eat at restaurants. Instead, Susan would beg her dad to take them to the airport to watch the airplanes take off and land. The colorful little propeller planes raced across the sky and came swooping in for landing. Susan fell in love with the airplanes and decided she really wanted to be a pilot. "But I'm a girl," she thought. "It seems unlikely that I can be a pilot."

Girls Can Be Smart

One day when Susan was in math class, she realized that she understood what the teacher was explaining. She looked around at all of her classmates, and everyone else, even the boys, seemed lost. "Hmm," she thought, "I kind of like math." Making all the numbers follow the rules made sense to Susan. She started getting good grades in her math classes. She knew that pilots needed to be good at math. Maybe it wasn't so unlikely that Susan could be a pilot after all.

Piloting an Airplane

When she was 15, Susan entered a speech contest at school where the winner got a free flying lesson. She worked very hard to give the best speech, and she won! Susan loved zipping around the skies, banking this way and that, and then landing on the runway just to take off again.

A New Dream

When she got her pilot's license, Susan discovered that she wanted to fly all kinds of different airplanes. She wanted to zoom higher and higher, and faster and faster. The fastest plane Susan knew about was the Space Shuttle, being built to fly in space. "Maybe I could fly in space," she began to hope. Then she told herself, "Nah, girls can't be astronauts. It's so unlikely."

Joining the Navy

Susan decided to join the Navy and learn to fly really fast jets. She still hoped to become an astronaut. Then one day, the most wonderful thing happened. A woman named Sally Ride flew on the Space Shuttle. Susan was so happy! But she didn't just want to fly on the Space Shuttle. She wanted to be the pilot. Since women were not allowed to train to be a Space Shuttle pilot, Susan's dream still felt unlikely.

A Trip to NASA

Finally, Susan got the chance to interview with NASA to become a Space Shuttle pilot. Three women interviewed for the job. Susan was the youngest and least experienced, so it was unlikely that she would be chosen. Susan had always worked hard, so she passed all the tests. Her interview went well, but she had to wait for months to find out if she would become a Space Shuttle pilot. She still thought it seemed unlikely that she would be chosen, but she was hopeful.

Unlikely Becomes Likely

Susan was zooming around the skies in her supersonic Navy jet when she got a radio call. NASA wanted to talk to her. "Well, I don't know what they're going to say, but at least the waiting is over," she thought. Susan nervously parked her jet. As she made the phone call, she held her breath. "Susan," the man on the phone said, "do you want to pilot the Space Shuttle?" Jumping for joy, Susan started yelling, "YES!"

Launching into Space

NASA chose Susan to fly the Space Shuttle. She trained hard for an entire year for the mission. In 1997, she launched into space as the second woman to ever pilot a Space Shuttle. Rocketing to space was thrilling!

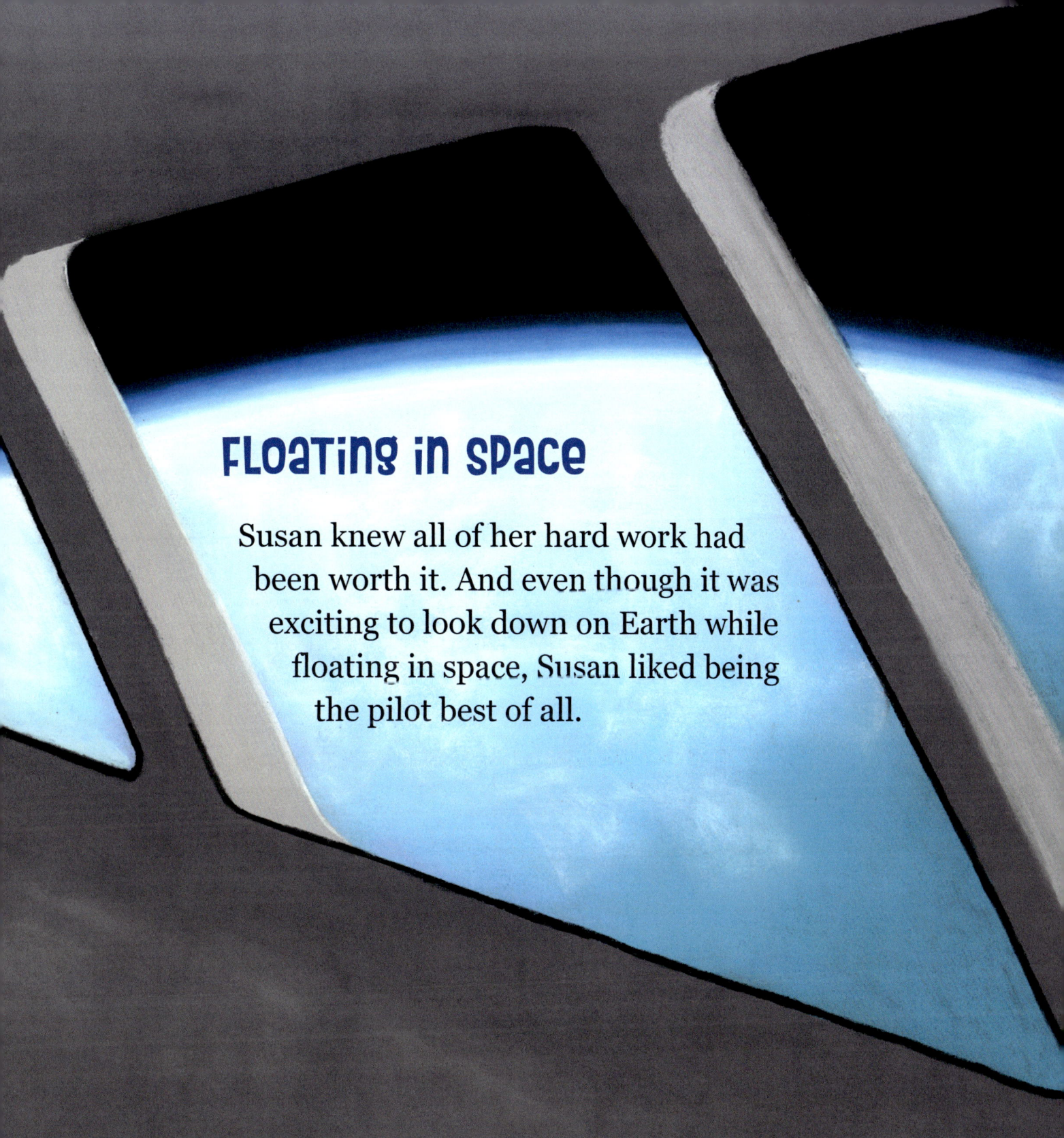

Floating in Space

Susan knew all of her hard work had been worth it. And even though it was exciting to look down on Earth while floating in space, Susan liked being the pilot best of all.

You can be something unlikely too

It was unlikely that Susan would grow up to be an astronaut – but she did. Maybe you want to do something unlikely. Maybe you think it is only a dream. If you work hard, you could make unlikely dreams come true, just like Susan. You might even travel to Mars one day!

words

Boisterous – noisy and full of energy

Convinced – you are sure that something is true

Propeller – the fan on an airplane that makes it move

Math – the study of numbers

Astronaut – a person who has been to space

Sally Ride – the first American woman to fly in space

NASA – the American space agency

Supersonic – faster than the speed of sound

Thrilling – exciting

Mars – another planet near Earth

Susan Kilrain

Commander Susan Kilrain is an astronaut, a Navy test pilot, an aerospace engineer, and a world traveler. She is the youngest person to pilot the space shuttle, and one of only three women to do so. She served twenty years in the Navy, paving the way for women along the way. She has flown more than 3,000 flight hours in over thirty different aircraft and was awarded the Defense Superior Service Medal. Susan piloted space shuttle missions STS-83 and STS-94, spending more than twenty days in space. When not training for a space flight, she worked in Mission Control during the launches and landings for other space shuttle missions. An avid photographer and astronomer, Susan is currently a motivational speaker, specializing in encouraging young women and underprivileged teens to excel in STEM careers. Learn more about her at www.susankilrain.com.

Becky Hardy

Becky Hardy is a self-taught artist who specializes in soft pastels and acrylics. Coming from a family of pilots and artists, her work is inspired by space exploration and the people behind the missions. Becky lives in Manchester in the United Kingdom, and when she's not in her art studio or working as a tax adviser, she is usually walking her dog or doing voluntary work. Learn more at www.artycosmos.com.

Francis French

Francis French is an educator, space historian, and bestselling author of space history books. This is his second children's book. Learn more at www.francisfrench.com.

An Unlikely Astronaut

Copyright © 2023 by Susan Kilrain.   All rights reserved.

No portion of this book may be reproduced, stored in a retrieval system, or transmitted in any form or by any means—electronic, mechanical, photocopy, recording, scanning, or other—except for brief quotations in critical reviews or articles, without prior written permission of the publisher. Requests to the publisher for permission, information, or questions concerning the book should be submitted via email to info@BookpressPublishing.com.

Published by: Bookpress Publishing • P.O. Box 71532, Des Moines, IA 50325 • www.BookpressPublishing.com

---

Publisher's Cataloging-in-Publication Data

Names: Kilrain, Susan, author. | French, Francis, author. | Hardy, Becky, illustrator.
Title: An Unlikely Astronaut / by Susan Kilrain; with Francis French; illustrated by Becky Hardy.
Description: Des Moines, IA: Bookpress Publishing, 2023. | Summary: The true story of how Astronaut Susan Kilrain overcame all obstacles to achieve her dream of flying in space when no American woman had.
Identifiers: LCCN: 2023940511 | ISBN: 978-1-947305-73-1
Subjects: LCSH Kilrain, Susan--Juvenile literature. | Astronauts--United States--Biography--Juvenile literature. | United States. National Aeronautics and Space Administration--Biography--Juvenile literature. | Women astronauts--United States--Biography--Juvenile literature. | BISAC JUVENILE NONFICTION / Biography & Autobiography / Science & Technology | JUVENILE NONFICTION / Biography & Autobiography / Women
Classification: LCC TL789.85.K55 2023 | DDC 629.450092--dc23

First Edition
Printed in the United States of America
10 9 8 7 6 5 4 3 2 1